Inside Voices

Leigh Ann Baka

BookLeaf Publishing

India | USA | UK

Presentation by *BookLeaf Publishing*

Web: www.bookleafpub.com

E-mail: info@bookleafpub.com

ISBN: 9789360949068

First edition 2024

DEDICATION

To my grandma, who always encouraged me to write.

To my family, who have loved me the whole time.

Depression

It's beige
like laying on the floor
in one spot
until you've melded in
and become a part of it

you can finally find the drive
to finally stand
but not to DO

it's the ringing silence
that can only crescendo
it's the single drop of rain
that ruins your page

it's empty
and dusty
and cavernous

and eternal.

Grama

The scent of lotion in the air
The steadfast whiteness of her hair
With two dogs
In her favorite rocking chair
The warm smells of cookies and tea

These are the things I bring with me

Bookstores and teapots
And owls galore
There isn't much else
A girl cold ask for

Words can't express what you mean to me

I'll never be the same
Once you leave me

Forever 23

I got a tattoo fo you the other day
Did you see it?
I saw a girl on the bus
thought she was you.
Swear to god I didn't know what to do
Lost my mind
It's been such a long time.
Those were the days we had –
Sittin' on the stoop all glad.
'Cause we had the good times
And we also rolled,
Running 'round with Lucy in the snow.
Sparkling sidewalks and gothic fountains.
These times I'll never forget.

Remember the days we were driving around
Shout-singing thru the window
At any stranger we found

I wish you were here
Because then

This poem wouldn't exist

me

qwerty keyboards are how we start
clicking and clacking
turning bytes into art

the sounds of the opera come out from above
the neighbors look up
not knowing what they heard

strangers walk past
they look at the trees
the rest of the city
won't ever have these

the music, it plays,
with a satisfying tune
whiling away days
staring up at the moon

hammocks and fires
and booze bottle art
these are the stories
that warm my heart

my time here never was
what we call free

but at least I learned
what it means to be me

goodbye for now

6

There was a time
when we were friends
I guess no one knows
how and when it will end

Decades we had
to dance in the yard
never knowing that
our part would be hard

I don't know
who was right
I don't know
if it matters

You'll always have
a place in my life
no matter how
words cut like a knife

memories together
can never change
one day, perhaps,
things will be the same

until then
my friend

I'll meet back with you

at our ends.

you again

She was my everything
she was my world
our entire life together
passed by in a whirl
i don't know what happened
don't know what went wrong
but something has broken
that can't be fixed with a song

the years in the yard
spent dancing routines
dreams splayed on the lawn
like an unfriendly tease
we drifted, it happens
that's not hard to see
what's hard is the way
that i couldn't be

there for you
like I thought
you were
there for me

Gardenias

9

Flowers in the garden
Flowers in the air
Flowers in the garden
Flowers everywhere

Evenings sometimes
Were filled with bats
Sometimes just moonvines
And playing with cats

Winters were filled
With lots of snow
Snowmen and Snowballs
Wherever we'd throw
Summers were filled
With lots of heat
Of fireworks and candy
It couldn't be beat
It's hard at the end
We've unfortunately seen
From loses and losses
All the things in between

One day you'll be happy
One day she'll be back

If only in heaven
Where she'll be her again

Flowers in the garden
Flowers in the air
Flowers in the garden

Surprise Trolley

the sight of lights off in the distance
the metal monster screeching closer
rounding the corner like a sad whale

bright lights shine from the top of the hill
the orange and white gives me such a thrill
metal on metal no matter how cold

head down to the tunnel
diving in to the ground
as others pass by us
their destinations unknown

rain

The rain poured today, but I didn't mind
swirling in circles that I like to find
cogs moving like clocks
in the windmills of my mind

it's hard know what's right
when you're feeling so wrong
like an unspoken poem
or an unwritten song

rain pounds on the window
it pours down in droves
like rivers filled with secrets
we'd all like to know

the words pour from inside in full verse
never knowing how true
or if it's the worst

the rain poured today
but I didn't mind

the rain poured today

and it was fine.

a mother's love

13

and a daughter's neglect

i've celebrated your joys

and mourned your losses

unfortunately it can be

too much to process

Paralyzed

have you ever had nightmares
not just bad dreams
the kinds that stay with you
even when you're awake

you open your eyes and see something great
but not in the good way – it just feels like hate
you try to scream but you can't
nothing, no sound, will come to your aid
what's that moving behind
'cause you can't turn around

alone in hotel rooms
asleep in the dark
you shouldn't be worried
it's safe, after all

until you remember -
there's no one to call
you came here alone

our fears disregard
the scariest parts of our dreams
until all that's left
is vast darkness and screams

Grief

Have you ever lost someone?
Do you know
how it feels?

Staring at the wall
feeling it all
remembering the dread you felt
in the first moments of the call

crashes and flashes and sickness to boot
feeling torn up from your bottom
from your root

it never gets easy
though you do get numb
and you'll never lose the feeling
of just wanting to run

away from the world and
away from it all

though nothing will help
to ease with the fall

downward and onward

and downward you go

until bottom is here
and you've nowhere to go

this is your new normal
you'll never go up

just hope it lays flat

it's no good when it's rough

Never Soon Enough

I can't say it anymore
Is that weird?
It almost comes out sometimes
and then -
I catch myself

What if?
When I say it again -
when I hear it again -
will it be another last?

What if?
I had said yes
Two weeks on the road
memories forever -

except -

suddenly -

you weren't there anymore.
they said it was too late
you told me you loved me

...then said, "I'll see you soon."

niceties

stop taking advantage and just leave me be
my kindness is gone and I'm not even me
i put in too much effort
with not enough back

i need this for me
i need myself back

it's been up
it's been down
you must really
hate this town

i wish you the best
you just can't stay
which is one of the hardest
things I've had to say

i believe there is more for you
i believe something good

i just don't know how to find it -
don't know that I could.

Inside Voices

hush!
do you hear it?

laughter from the hallway
as she cries out to you
she doesn't need help

crash!
was that the storm?

now there's crying down there
don't you hear it

it's scary
no,
it's Baby

hush!
don't you get it?

it's only a storm, we will be okay
the dog will stop crying
once it goes away

now, go back down the hall way

and into your room
the tickling that stopped
will start again soon

flash!
did you see it?

the lights came back on
and we're all okay
sometimes that happens

in trailers, anyway

In the end

I got closer than I thought

And that's enough

23

for now.